Agentic AI

Harnessing the Power of Autonomous Systems in the Modern Workplace

Taylor Royce

DEDICATION

All of the pioneers, visionaries, and inventors who are influencing the direction of technology are honored in this book. To the leaders, thinkers, and dreamers who are dedicated to using artificial intelligence to make the world a better, smarter, and more efficient place, and to those who rise to the challenge of pushing the limits of what is possible.

I hope this work encourages and equips you to investigate the enormous possibilities of agentic AI and take the lead in changing the workplace for future generations.

CONTENTS

ACKNOWLEDGMENTS

I want to express my sincere gratitude to everyone who helped to make this book possible.

To my family, for your constant encouragement and support during this journey. Your understanding, patience, and faith in me have been tremendous.

To my colleagues and mentors, whose knowledge and perceptions in the field of artificial intelligence have greatly influenced and inspired the content found here. I have gained a greater understanding of this ever changing profession thanks in large part to your teaching.

I would especially like to thank the beta testers and early readers who helped me improve and solidify this work by offering insightful criticism. Your well-considered recommendations made sure that this book not only imparts knowledge but also strikes a chord with readers.

I am thankful to the groups of academics, practitioners, and developers who are putting in endless effort to make agentic AI a reality. Your innovative work keeps pushing the limits of what AI is capable of.

Lastly, I would like to express my gratitude to all of the readers who will be delving into this book for their interest and dedication to learning about the future of autonomous systems. I sincerely hope that this work gives you the information and motivation you need to seize the opportunities presented by agentic AI and take the lead in revolutionizing the workplace.

You own this book just as much as I do.

CHAPTER 1

Overview of Artificial Intelligence

1.1 Agentic AI: Definition and Application

Artificial intelligence endowed with agency, or agentic AI, describes systems that are capable of independent goal-pursuit, environment adaptation, and decision-making. Agentic AI possesses the ability to comprehend, learn, and act based on the information it receives, which is similar to the characteristics of human agency, in contrast to traditional, rule-based AI that needs pre-defined instructions. Because of this agency, it is able to perform proactive and adaptive actions to accomplish particular objectives, going beyond reactive duties.

Agentic artificial intelligence has a wide range of applications that call for flexibility, judgment, and self-directed behavior. Intelligent digital assistants that customize user experiences, sophisticated robotics that

2

manage intricate jobs, and autonomous cars that must react to erratic road conditions are a few examples. In addition to responding, these systems are made to anticipate demands, learn from encounters, and adjust their course of action in response to fresh information and changing circumstances.

Important domains under the realm of agentic AI encompass:

- **Autonomous Decision-Making:** Systems that make decisions on their own without continual human supervision by analyzing circumstances, weighing possibilities, and choosing courses of action.

- **Adaptive Learning:** Algorithms that can improve their performance over time by changing their behavior in response to new input.

AI agents that pursue specific goals and are able to adjust their strategy as necessary to achieve them, even in the face of changing circumstances, are said to exhibit goal-oriented behavior.

In order to make morally and socially responsible decisions in crucial situations, such as healthcare or security, certain agentic AI is being developed with inbuilt ethical frameworks.

To fully appreciate how this form of intelligence is developing to assist, improve, and occasionally challenge human autonomy and decision-making, it is imperative to comprehend the definition and application of agentic AI.

1.2 Essential Qualities and Skills

Agentic AI differs from traditional AI due to a number of unique features and capabilities. These characteristics allow it to function in dynamic settings, manage challenging assignments, and, in certain situations, collaborate or even function independently without requiring a lot of human involvement.

The salient features of agentic AI are as follows:

- **Autonomy:** The capacity to act on one's own initiative in complicated situations, adhering to predetermined goals or changing course when necessary. AI autonomy involves less reliance on human input to make decisions.

- The machine learning models that agentic AI systems are outfitted with enable them to process vast amounts of data, identify trends, and modify their behavior in response to experience. With the use of this skill, they can "learn" from previous encounters and gradually improve their answers.

- **Intentionality and Goal Orientation:** These systems function according to predefined goals, making choices to achieve them. Agentic AI has an internal drive (goal-oriented programming) that directs its behavior toward reaching predetermined goals, in contrast to reactive AI, which reacts to stimuli without a larger purpose.

- **Context Awareness:** Agentic AI systems are built to comprehend the environment in which they function, enabling them to make complex choices depending on contextual elements. A medical AI system might, for instance, customize its suggestions according to the patient's medical history and present health indicators.

- **Problem-Solving Abilities:** These systems are able to assess a variety of possible courses of action, forecast probable results, and choose the most effective one to accomplish their objectives. They can successfully and frequently in real-time manage unforeseen circumstances because of this capability.

- **Interaction and Cooperation:** In order to accomplish a common objective, agentic AI frequently communicates, shares information, and occasionally engages in negotiation with humans or other AI systems. These teamwork abilities are essential in fields like robotics, healthcare, and finance.

With applications in domains that demand flexibility, foresight, and interactive decision-making, agentic AI is a revolutionary force thanks to the confluence of these qualities. These systems will probably grow much more adept at integrating themselves into settings where they can carry out complex, contextually aware activities as technology develops.

1.3 AI's Development Towards Agency

There have been notable developments in computing power, machine learning methods, and data accessibility along the transition from basic rule-based systems to agentic AI. AI was first developed as a way to automate repetitive, specialized operations that had to adhere to rigid standards. But as technology developed and industry demands increased, AI developed to play increasingly complicated jobs requiring flexibility, judgment, and even reasoning.

Important stages in AI's development toward agency include:

1. Rule-Based Systems: Early artificial intelligence was quite deterministic, producing predictable results based on predetermined input patterns by following preset instructions. Despite their efficiency, these systems lacked adaptation and flexibility.

2. Machine Learning and Pattern Recognition: As machine learning advances, AI systems may be able to identify patterns in data and use that knowledge to enhance their performance. With this development, AI became less inflexible and could process a wider range of data inputs, including speech and image recognition.

3. Deep Learning and Neural Networks: The development of neural networks and deep learning algorithms greatly expanded the potential of artificial intelligence, particularly in domains requiring intricate data processing. By simulating neural architecture in the human brain, these models allowed systems to attain great accuracy in tasks like language processing and image classification.

4. Reinforcement Learning: Agentic AI has been made possible in large part by reinforcement learning, in which systems learn by being rewarded or punished for their activities. Applications in game theory, robotics, and other fields can result from AI agents' ability to independently learn methods that optimize long-term gains through trial and error.

5. Multi-Agent Systems and Collaborative AI:

Multi-agent systems, in which several AI agents cooperate and communicate to accomplish common goals, represent the most recent stage in the development of AI. Large-scale simulations, distributed problem-solving, and swarm robots all depend on this collaborative intelligence.

The development of fully agentic AI, which combines autonomy, contextual awareness, goal orientation, and learning capabilities, is the pinnacle of these developments. In addition to being responsive, this type of AI is capable of actively contributing to decision-making and problem-solving in challenging real-world situations.

The desire for more intelligent, flexible, and independent systems has propelled AI's development towards agency. This trend bridges the gap between artificial systems and human-like agency by reflecting our growing dependence on AI for tasks requiring complex problem-solving skills and autonomous decision-making.

CHAPTER 2

THE FUNDAMENTAL TECHNOLOGIES THAT MAKE AGENTIC AI POSSIBLE

2.1 Models of Self-Governing Planning and Decision-Making

The ability of agentic AI to make decisions on its own, which is a difficult task requiring advanced planning and decision-making models, is its fundamental component. AI agents may define objectives, predict future conditions, evaluate several options, and choose the best course of action to accomplish desired results thanks to autonomous planning and decision-making models. These features are crucial for a variety of applications, from advanced analytics and tailored recommendations to robotics and driverless cars.

Several essential elements are necessary for autonomous planning and decision-making:

- The AI system needs to initially be assigned a goal, which could be anything from navigating a physical location to tailoring a user's experience to their preferences. Systems must adapt to new information as it becomes available, and goals can be either static or dynamic.

- **Perception and Situational Awareness:** The AI needs to correctly perceive its surroundings in order to make wise decisions. In order to provide a depiction of the current state of affairs, this entails collecting data from sensors, user inputs, or other external sources.

- **Prediction and Simulation:** In order to predict the possible results of certain actions, advanced decision-making models frequently use predictive modeling to simulate numerous scenarios. This enables AI systems to assess potential outcomes and reduce risks, which is particularly helpful in unexpected circumstances.

- **Optimization and Utility Maximization:** Agentic AI systems evaluate and rank actions according to the probability of reaching the best result in accordance with predetermined goals. They assess several courses of action using optimization algorithms and select the one that maximizes utility or strikes the optimal balance between conflicting objectives.

- In autonomous planning, reinforcement learning in which an AI agent learns by interacting with its surroundings is essential. It can gradually improve its decision-making procedures by using feedback from trial and error in the form of incentives or sanctions.

- **Hierarchical Planning:** AI may use hierarchical planning to break down difficult tasks into smaller tasks or sub-goals. This method increases productivity and enables the system to manage multi-step procedures or adjust to conditions that change at each stage.

Agentic AI can act with purpose and adaptability thanks to these autonomous planning and decision-making models. These qualities are crucial for intelligent systems in unexpected or mission-critical applications including financial analysis, robotic navigation, and healthcare diagnostics.

2.2 Natural language processing and advanced machine learning

The basis for the learning, comprehension, and adaptation of agentic AI is advanced machine learning (ML) and natural language processing (NLP) technologies. Agentic AI systems can now evaluate enormous volumes of data, identify patterns, and modify their behavior in response to new information thanks to these technologies. For an AI system to interpret a variety of data kinds, engage in meaningful human interaction, and continuously enhance its performance, machine learning and natural language processing are essential.

Among these technologies' salient features are:

- **Supervised and Unsupervised Learning:** In supervised learning, labeled datasets are used to teach agentic AI systems to identify particular correlations or patterns. Conversely, unsupervised learning enables AI to examine data without predetermined classifications, revealing insights and patterns that are otherwise concealed. Building intelligent systems that can identify things, decipher photos, or suggest tailored information starts with these methods.

- **Neural networks and deep learning:** Remarkable levels of accuracy in speech and picture identification, natural language processing, and decision-making have been made possible by neural networks, especially deep learning models. Agentic AI can manage complicated datasets because of deep learning architectures like convolutional neural networks (CNNs) and recurrent neural networks (RNNs). This allows computers to comprehend language, interpret visual information, and identify emotions in voices.

- The ability of agentic AI to process, comprehend, and react to human language is made possible by natural language processing (NLP). Building conversational agents, virtual assistants, and other applications that call for human-AI interaction requires this skill. Machine translation, named entity recognition, and sentiment analysis are examples of advanced NLP approaches. Furthermore, advancements like transformers and language models like GPT and BERT have greatly improved natural language processing (NLP), enabling agentic AI systems to comprehend context, produce logical answers, and even demonstrate empathy during conversations.

- **Reinforcement Learning and Transfer Learning:** As was already established, agentic AI can improve its decisions over time through reinforcement learning. Another crucial strategy is transfer learning, in which an AI model that has been trained on one task is used to complete a related task using less training data. Because AI systems can "transfer" learned information to similar settings without having to start from scratch, deploying them in new environments is made easier and faster.

- **Data Processing and Feature Engineering:** To transform unprocessed inputs into a format that models can comprehend, advanced machine learning depends on data processing. Specifically, feature engineering entails choosing and altering pertinent data features to enhance model performance and accuracy. Effective data processing guarantees that agentic AI systems may learn effectively from a variety of data sources, including unstructured data (such as text and images) and structured data (such as databases).

Agentic AI's capacity to comprehend unstructured material, communicate with people, and learn from experience is largely dependent on machine learning and natural language processing. Because of these technologies, agentic AI systems can analyze data, offer insights, and even have meaningful conversations that change based on the needs of the user.

2.3 Cloud computing and IoT integration

For agentic AI to operate at scale and in real-time across distributed contexts, integration with cloud computing and the Internet of Things (IoT) is essential. By giving access to enormous volumes of data, facilitating real-time processing, and facilitating distributed intelligence across several devices, the Internet of Things and cloud computing combine to increase the potential of agentic AI.

Important components of this integration consist of:

- **Data Collection and Real-Time Processing:** Sensors, cameras, and other connected devices produce constant streams of data for IoT devices. As demonstrated by applications like smart homes, industrial automation, and predictive maintenance, agentic AI can interpret real-time data from these sources by interacting with the Internet of Things. This enables quick responses to environmental changes.

- **Scalability and Flexibility:** A key component of agentic AI, cloud computing offers the infrastructure required to store and handle massive datasets. AI systems can undertake complicated analyses, serve more users, and manage larger datasets without major delays or hardware limitations by utilizing cloud resources to expand their computational capacity according to demand.

- **Edge computing and distributed intelligence:** By processing data close to its source (on local servers or Internet of Things devices, for example), edge computing eliminates the requirement for data to be sent to a central cloud server. This dispersed intelligence enables agentic AI to make localized decisions more quickly and effectively, especially in settings with poor connectivity. Applications where low latency is essential, such as remote monitoring and driverless cars, benefit greatly from edge computing.

- Important concerns regarding data privacy and security are brought up by the integration of agentic

AI with cloud computing and the Internet of Things. Implementing safe data management procedures is crucial because sensitive data moves between devices, edge servers, and the cloud. To safeguard data and guarantee that agentic AI systems abide by data privacy laws, sophisticated encryption, anonymization, and access control procedures are required.

- **Interoperability and Connectivity:** Interoperability is essential for agentic AI to function flawlessly with cloud services and IoT devices. Effective communication between various systems is made possible by standardized protocols, APIs, and integration frameworks, which promote seamless data flow and reliable performance across a range of platforms and devices.

Across a variety of industries, this combination of agentic AI, IoT, and cloud computing opens up new possibilities for autonomous, responsive, and connected systems. The convergence of these technologies gives agentic AI the reach, scalability, and processing capacity it requires to function well in a complex, data-rich world, from assisting predictive analytics in healthcare to enabling real-time decision-making in smart cities.

CHAPTER 3

USING AGENTIC AI IN PRACTICE: USE CASES AND APPLICATIONS

3.1 Using Agentic AI for Support and Customer Service

Customer service has changed as a result of agentic AI's ability to provide individualized, effective, and highly interactive experiences through a variety of channels. Agentic AI systems, which range from chatbots and virtual assistants to intelligent contact centers, improve customer service by making judgments in real time, picking up on interactions, and reacting accurately and empathetically.

The following are some of the main advantages and capabilities of agentic AI in customer service:

- **24/7 Availability and Instant Response:** AI-driven customer support representatives work around the clock to provide assistance. They can answer questions right away, guaranteeing that clients receive help promptly and cutting down on wait times considerably. This is particularly beneficial for multinational companies with a wide-ranging, widely-spread clientele.

- **Personalized and Contextual encounters**: To create a more individualized experience, agentic AI customizes responses based on information from previous encounters, prior purchases, and consumer profiles. Whether addressing a complaint, offering advice, or helping with a transaction, agentic AI can dynamically modify its tone and approach by examining the intent, sentiment, and context of the client.

- **Natural Language Processing (NLP) for Improved Communication**: Agentic AI systems can comprehend and produce human language with a high level of accuracy and fluency thanks to NLP technology. Chatbots and virtual assistants with natural language processing (NLP) capabilities can comprehend intricate consumer inquiries, give precise answers, and even refer problems to human agents when needed. This language competence raises client happiness and increases communication quality overall.

- **Proactive Engagement and Issue Resolution:** By anticipating customers' demands based on data insights, agentic AI may engage with customers proactively in addition to providing reactive help. An AI assistant might, for example, notify clients of new product developments, remind them of impending payments, or offer assistance in utilizing a service. Agentic AI promotes brand loyalty and improves the consumer experience by anticipating and resolving possible problems.

- **Scalability and Cost Efficiency:** Agentic AI systems are extremely scalable solutions for companies of all sizes since they can manage thousands of client interactions at once. Because businesses can lessen their reliance on human agents while still providing excellent customer service, this scalability results in huge cost savings.

- **Continuous Learning and Improvement:** Agentic AI systems continuously get better thanks to machine learning, which uses feedback and previous interactions. Over time, they adjust to manage a greater variety of inquiries, examine trends in client interactions, and learn from successful results. With every client interaction, agentic AI gets more effective and efficient because of this ongoing development.

Customer service applications of agentic AI have changed how companies communicate with their customers by developing support systems that are quicker, easier to use, and more effective. These AI-powered technologies help businesses by optimizing resources and improving operational efficiency, in addition to providing end users with better customer experiences.

3.2 Process automation and business operations

Agentic AI is transforming process automation in business operations by allowing intelligent, self-governing systems that improve operational efficiency, decrease manual intervention, and streamline workflows. Agentic AI is improving many aspects of corporate operations, from human resources to supply chain management, increasing an organization's agility and responsiveness.

The following are some key uses and benefits of agentic AI in corporate operations:

- **Intelligent Workflow Automation**: Agentic AI is capable of dynamically analyzing processes, making judgments, and carrying out actions, whereas traditional automation solutions rely on static rules. An AI system in HR, for example, may independently screen resumes, set up interviews, and follow up with candidates. It can also modify its strategy in response to candidate input and the particular job needs. High-volume activities become more efficient thanks to this clever automation, which also decreases the need for human intervention in repeated tasks.

- **Predictive Analytics for Decision Support**: To

assist in making decisions in intricate situations, agentic AI makes use of predictive analytics. Agentic AI systems can forecast demand, optimize inventory, and identify possible operational risks by examining past data and trends. For example, AI systems in manufacturing may predict when equipment will break and plan maintenance in advance, reducing downtime and increasing efficiency.

- **AI-Enhanced Robotic Process Automation (RPA):** Conventional RPA manages repetitive, organized tasks, but it frequently has trouble with unstructured data. RPA's capabilities are increased by agentic AI, which adds flexibility and intelligent decision-making. AI-enhanced RPA, for instance, may process invoices, validate data across several systems, and manage exceptions without the need for human interaction, outperforming traditional RPA alone in terms of speed and accuracy.

- **Supply Chain Optimization:** By evaluating supplier, logistical, and inventory data, agentic AI plays a key role in streamlining supply chain operations. In order to effectively satisfy demand, AI-driven systems can modify procurement plans, control inventory levels, and organize logistics. They guarantee smooth operations by reacting instantly to changes, such as shifts in demand or interruptions in the supply chain.

- **Financial Process Automation:** Agentic AI in finance automates processes such as credit rating, fraud detection, and accounts reconciliation. Agentic AI can identify irregularities by examining trends in financial data, highlighting possible credit problems or fraudulent activity. Finance departments can react quickly to any anomalies because to this real-time monitoring and decision-making power, shielding the company from monetary loss and harm to its brand.

- **Enhanced Customer Relationship Management (CRM):** AI-powered CRM platforms provide useful information about the preferences, behavior, and possible needs of customers. Businesses can customize their marketing and sales tactics for each individual consumer by using agentic AI to assess interactions across many touchpoints. Agentic AI improves customer happiness and boosts income by automating replies and streamlining outreach initiatives.

The incorporation of agentic AI into corporate processes has resulted in revolutionary shifts in consumer engagement, cost effectiveness, and productivity. AI-powered solutions enable businesses to function at a scale and level of accuracy that would be unattainable with conventional techniques by performing complicated jobs and making wise judgments on their own.

3.3 Medical and Healthcare Autonomous Systems

Agentic AI is revolutionizing healthcare by assisting physicians, improving patient care, and streamlining hospital operations. Agentic AI is used by autonomous healthcare systems to give care more effectively, with real-time insights and customized treatment plans. With great promise to improve patient outcomes and accessibility, this technology is improving the clinical and administrative aspects of healthcare.

The following are some uses and effects of agentic AI in healthcare:

- **Medical Imaging Analysis and Diagnosis:** Agentic AI is particularly strong in medical imaging, where it can accurately identify disorders by autonomously analyzing CT, MRI, and X-ray data. AI-driven imaging technologies help radiologists by pointing out trouble spots, spotting anomalies like tumors or fractures, and even making recommendations for potential diagnoses. Agentic AI enhances patient care and facilitates early intervention by expediting and improving diagnosis accuracy.

- **Personalized Treatment Plans:** To customize treatment regimens for each patient, personalized medicine uses data-driven insights. To recommend the best course of treatment, agentic AI examines patient data, such as genetic information, medical history, and lifestyle choices. To increase the efficacy of treatment, an AI system might, for example, suggest a particular chemotherapy regimen based on the genetic profile of a patient's cancer.

- **Telemedicine with Remote Patient Monitoring:** In remote monitoring, agentic AI is essential for tracking patient vitals and identifying any early indicators of decline by evaluating data from wearable technology and other sensors. AI systems can notify healthcare professionals to take action before a minor problem worsens by continuously monitoring patients, particularly those with chronic diseases. In telemedicine, where patients can receive prompt care from the convenience of their homes, this proactive approach is crucial.

- **medication Discovery and Development:** By evaluating intricate biological data and spotting potential molecules, the pharmaceutical sector is utilizing agentic AI to speed up medication discovery. Researchers can concentrate on the most promising possibilities by using AI models to forecast how novel medications will affect human biology. It is possible to launch novel medicines more quickly thanks to this data-driven strategy, which cuts down on development cycle expenses and time.

- **Hospital and Resource Management:** AI-powered solutions manage staffing, equipment, and bed distribution to maximize hospital operations. Hospitals may better manage resources, cut down on wait times, and guarantee that crucial care is always accessible by using agentic AI to estimate patient inflow. To further streamline operations, AI technologies also help automate administrative duties like arranging appointments and billing.

- **Mental Health and Wellness:** The use of agentic AI is growing in the field of mental health care, where monitoring tools and virtual therapists provide easily available assistance for people dealing with mental health issues. Chatbots with artificial intelligence (AI) serve users with mild to moderate symptoms by offering cognitive behavioral therapy (CBT) methods and other mental health resources.

Particularly in places where traditional services are few, these tools provide a new degree of accessibility to mental health care.

A new era of accuracy, accessibility, and efficiency is being ushered in by the use of agentic AI in healthcare. Agentic AI has the ability to improve healthcare delivery and make high-quality care available to a larger population by automating repetitive chores, offering sophisticated diagnostic insights, and customizing treatment alternatives.

CHAPTER 4

CREATING AGENTIC AI SYSTEMS

The process of creating agentic AI systems is intricate and iterative, requiring a blend of technical precision, strategic forethought, and flexibility. These systems are characterized by their capacity to learn from their surroundings, act independently toward predetermined objectives, and make decisions based on ongoing feedback. To guarantee that the final agent is not only functional but also flexible, resilient, and moral, every step in the development of agentic AI systems must be carefully planned and carried out.

4.1 How to Create AI Agents with Goals

Developing goal-driven AI agents entails building machines that can navigate challenging situations on their own to accomplish predetermined goals. To establish the objectives, identify the required steps, and facilitate independent decision-making, the design process necessitates a systematic method. Important actions consist of:

- **Outlining Goals and Purpose:** Any goal-driven AI agent's development starts with a precise description of the main goals and parameters of the system. This entails determining the intended results, the limitations the agent must work under, and the success indicators. By establishing limits for the agent's behaviors, concentrating on particular tasks, and minimizing needless complexity, scope definition aids in development guidance.

- **Environment Analysis:** Developing successful AI solutions requires an understanding of the environment in which the agent will function. This entails examining the agent's digital or physical environment, seeing possible problems, and determining if pertinent data is readily available. Developers can foresee challenges, plan for different scenarios, and create paths that the agent might follow to accomplish its objectives by modeling the environment.

- **Selection of Action and Development of Strategy**: Goal-driven agents need to have a set of behaviors they can use depending on the circumstances they find themselves in. Choosing the right course of action entails determining the tactics that will influence the agent's behavior and assessing how each course of action fits in with the overall goals. Algorithms like reinforcement learning, which allow the agent to learn by making mistakes and eventually improving its strategy, are frequently used in action-selection systems.

- **Creating Frameworks for Decision-Making:** A goal-driven AI agent has to have decision-making frameworks that enable it to select from a variety of possible courses of action. Neural networks, logic-based decision trees, and probabilistic models are frequently included in these frameworks. A healthcare AI agent might, for instance, employ a decision-making framework to select among several treatment alternatives in light of patient information, medical recommendations, and risk factors. The agent's ability to react to intricate and changing circumstances is guaranteed by this skill.

- **Putting Motivation and Reward Systems in Place:** In order to direct an agent's behavior and reinforce behaviors that lead to the accomplishment of goals, reward mechanisms are crucial. Developers can influence the agent's decision-making process and encourage it to prioritize particular behaviors over others by establishing rewards and punishments for particular activities. To connect its behavior with company objectives, an AI agent in supply chain management, for example, might be given a "reward" for cutting delivery times or improving inventory levels.

- **Training and Simulation:** Developers frequently test and improve the performance of AI agents in simulations prior to implementing them in real-world settings. With the use of simulations, an agent can experiment with various acts, adjust to criticism, and gain knowledge from its experiences without fear of repercussions in the actual world. Developers may make sure that agents are prepared to manage the complexity and unpredictability of their intended surroundings by training them in simulated scenarios.

A methodical and systematic strategy that strikes a balance between accuracy and adaptability is necessary for designing goal-driven AI agents. Every stage of the design process builds on the one before it, creating an agent that can behave autonomously and with purpose in dynamic and frequently difficult situations.

4.2 Creating Feedback Loops That Adapt

The foundation of agentic AI is feedback loops, which allow systems to continuously improve their performance in response to changing circumstances and real-time input. AI agents can learn from their past behavior, modify their behavior, and stay responsive to environmental changes by using adaptive feedback systems. The following are crucial elements of creating adaptive feedback loops:

- **Real-Time Data Gathering and Tracking:** Continuous data gathering is necessary for adaptive feedback loops in order to track the agent's actions and the results they generate. The system may learn about its performance, spot trends, and spot irregularities thanks to real-time monitoring. The agent can adjust its activities based on this data, which becomes the basis for assessing how effective its judgments were.

- **Mechanisms for Error Detection and Correction:** An AI agent needs to be able to recognize and fix mistakes on its own in order to adapt successfully. This process entails determining when an action has unintended repercussions or when a goal is not being met. While correction mechanisms modify the agent's approach to lessen or rectify the error, error-detection mechanisms frequently employ anomaly detection algorithms and predictive models to foresee problems before they become more serious.

- Learning from Historical Data Adaptive feedback

loops use past data to guide present-day choices. The agent can find effective tactics, steer clear of prior blunders, and enhance overall performance by examining past actions and results. To improve its strategy for upcoming interactions, an agent in a customer service application, for example, can examine previous exchanges to identify which answers result in greater pleasure.

- **Behavioral Adjustment and Parameter Tuning**: Mechanisms for modifying the agent's behavior in response to feedback are necessary for an adaptive feedback loop. This could entail updating the agent's reward system, changing decision thresholds, or fine-tuning settings. For instance, in reaction to shifting road conditions, feedback loops in autonomous cars can modify variables like speed, braking distance, and lane position to maximize safety and fuel efficiency.

- **Continuous Improvement through Reinforcement Learning:** Reinforcement learning is a potent method for creating AI agents that are adaptive. The agent can enhance its decision-making process iteratively by interacting with the environment and getting feedback in the form of rewards or penalties. With the use of reinforcement learning models, such Q-learning and policy gradient approaches, the agent can gradually improve its performance by optimizing its behavior.

- **HiTL (Human-in-the-Loop) for Improved Feedback**: Adaptive feedback loops may occasionally involve human interaction to offer further supervision or direction. Human operators can analyze the agent's choices, offer corrections, or improve the feedback criteria with human-in-the-loop systems. HITL is particularly useful in high-stakes applications where human knowledge may supplement and improve the AI's learning process, such as financial trading or medical diagnostics.

Developing agentic AI systems that can continuously evolve and improve requires adaptive feedback loops. Developers may guarantee that AI agents stay responsive, adaptable, and in line with their intended goals by integrating systems for real-time data collecting, mistake correction, and reinforcement learning.

4.3 Evaluation, Testing, and Iterative Development

In order to ensure that agentic AI systems fulfill performance requirements, follow moral principles, and are ready to function securely in real-world scenarios, testing and evaluation are crucial phases in the development process. Testing and assessment must be thorough, iterative, and data-driven due to the dynamic and complicated nature of agentic AI. Important components of this procedure consist of:

- **Establishing Evaluation Criteria and Success Metrics:** Establishing precise success measures is the initial stage in evaluating an agentic AI system. Accuracy, efficiency, safety, ethical alignment, and user pleasure are a few examples of these measures. An AI system for medical diagnosis, for example, may be assessed according to patient safety, medical ethics compliance, and diagnostic accuracy.

Developers can systematically assess the agent's performance and pinpoint opportunities for development by defining these criteria.

- **Simulated Testing settings:** Before deploying the agent, developers can test its performance in a controlled environment by using simulated settings. Through situations that test the agent's abilities and decision-making processes, simulations mimic real-world circumstances. This method works especially well for complicated applications where real-world testing could provide logistical or safety problems, including autonomous driving or industrial automation.

- **Edge case analysis and scenario-based testing:** Agentic AI systems need to be capable of managing a variety of situations, including uncommon or harsh ones. While edge case research looks at how the agent behaves in odd or unexpected situations, scenario-based testing exposes the agent to a variety of scenarios. An autonomous car might be tested, for example, in situations with rapid weather changes, unexpected roadblocks, or erratic pedestrian behavior. The agent's resilience and dependability under a variety of circumstances are guaranteed by this testing.

- **Ethics and Bias Evaluation:** AI systems need to be assessed for ethical issues, including decision-making fairness and possible biases. Any underlying biases in the data or algorithms that might provide biased results should be found through testing. The ethical ramifications of the agent's behaviors must also be taken into account by developers, particularly in applications like criminal justice, healthcare, and employment that have an impact on people's lives. Developing ethical AI systems requires minimizing prejudice and guaranteeing equity.

- **Usability testing and user acceptance testing (UAT):** By analyzing the agent's performance from the viewpoint of the end user, user acceptance testing determines whether it fulfills user expectations and provides a positive experience.

Conversely, usability testing concentrates on the agent's usability, accessibility, and interface. Developers can get input on the agent's usability, functionality, and practical significance by including end users in the testing process.

- **Version control and iterative improvement:** Testing and evaluation are components of a continuous process of improvement rather than one-time events. Iterative improvement entails introducing improvements, retesting the system to gauge progress, and improving the agent in response to testing feedback. By ensuring that every iteration is recorded, version control enables developers to keep track of modifications, roll back to earlier iterations when needed, and document the agent's development.

- **Post-Deployment Maintenance and Monitoring**: Continuous monitoring is crucial to track the agent's performance, handle any new problems that arise, and make the required modifications after it is deployed in a real-world setting. Developers can find areas where the agent might need more training or fine-tuning through post-deployment monitoring. Over time, maintenance makes sure the agent stays secure, operational, and in line with its original objectives.

Testing, assessment, and iterative development are critical to the success of agentic AI systems. Developers may ensure AI bots are prepared to operate effectively, morally, and in line with human values by employing rigorous testing, scenario analysis, moral evaluation, and continuous improvement.

CHAPTER 5

THE VIRTUAL WORKFORCE: THE IMPACT OF AGENTIC AI ON WORKPLACE TRANSFORMATION

Through the introduction of a "virtual workforce" that can perform a wide range of jobs independently, agentic AI is altering conventional labor structures. This change represents a significant change in labor dynamics and affects how businesses function, assign tasks, and interact with their workforce. Agentic AI enables companies to attain previously unheard-of levels of efficiency, responsiveness, and innovation through work offloading, productivity increase, and role redefining.

5.1 Human Augmentation and Task Offloading

Agentic Because AI can handle difficult tasks on its own, businesses may free up human workers to concentrate on high-value, strategic work by offloading repetitive and time-consuming jobs. Human augmentation and task offloading are examples of a cooperative synergy between AI and human workers, where each enhances the other's skills and talents.

Agentic AI is particularly good at automating mundane and repetitive operations that take up valuable employee time. Data input, document processing, and workflow management are a few examples of these duties. AI agents can drastically cut down on human workloads by taking over certain duties, increasing operational effectiveness and lowering burnout. AI chatbots, for instance, may answer routine customer service questions, freeing up human workers to handle delicate or complicated problems.

Using Data Insights to Support Decision-Making: The capacity of agentic AI to evaluate enormous data volumes and derive useful insights is among its most potent uses. Large volumes of data may be processed rapidly by AI agents, which can then spot trends, patterns, and anomalies that human workers might miss. Agentic AI supports human decision-making by offering data-driven suggestions, assisting staff members in making better decisions. For example, AI-driven analysis in financial services might direct investment strategies by pointing out risk elements or new market trends.

Augmenting Creative and Analytical Skills: By producing insights, evaluating possibilities, and even helping with idea generation, AI can assist human creativity and analytical activities. AI systems, for instance, can evaluate customer data in marketing to recommend the best content strategies or focused advertising tactics. Similar to this, AI-powered tools can help with iterative testing and optimization in product design, giving designers more freedom to experiment.

Enabling Problem-Solving and Real-Time Assistance: Agentic AI supports human workers in real time, especially in settings where quick reactions are essential. AI systems, for instance, can help doctors in the healthcare industry by making recommendations in real time based on patient information, previous medical records, and professional guidelines. This instant assistance improves judgment and lowers the possibility of mistakes, particularly in high-stakes scenarios.

By allowing workers to concentrate on intricate, innovative, and strategic tasks, task offloading and human augmentation radically change the nature of work. As a flexible and industrious helper, agentic AI may do a range of support tasks, freeing up staff members to use their knowledge where it is most useful.

5.2 Using Autonomous Systems to Increase Productivity

The autonomous capabilities of agentic AI are revolutionizing productivity norms in several industries by increasing efficiency, optimizing resources, and simplifying procedures. Agentic AI raises productivity and establishes new standards for operational performance by allowing systems to function with little assistance from humans.

Optimizing Resource Allocation: Agentic AI systems are able to allocate resources in real-time, where they are most needed, using dynamic resource management. AI-driven technologies, for instance, may track inventory levels, demand trends, and supply chain interruptions in logistics and supply chain management, enabling businesses to make preemptive resource adjustments. This optimization guarantees that resources are used effectively, cuts down on waste, and minimizes delays, all of which increase production.

Improving Workflow Efficiency: Agentic AI can decrease process bottlenecks and optimize operations by automating workflows. Schedules, approvals, and compliance checks are just a few of the many jobs that automated systems manage, enabling workflows to move forward without requiring human interaction. AI-powered solutions in the finance industry may handle compliance, process transactions, and validate financial data, speeding up labor-intensive and time-consuming procedures.

Predictive maintenance and decreased downtime are made possible by: AI systems keep an eye on machinery and equipment in the manufacturing and industrial sectors to forecast maintenance requirements. AI agents assist in minimizing downtime, enhancing asset reliability, and preserving production by seeing possible problems before they result in equipment failure. By reducing operational disruptions, predictive maintenance preserves uninterrupted productivity while saving money and time.

Reducing Error Rates through Machine Precision: AI systems are extremely dependable for tasks requiring accuracy and consistency since they are not prone to fatigue or attention like human workers are. AI can lower error rates and produce higher-quality results by automating intricate and meticulous processes. AI can analyze data with remarkable precision in domains like pharmaceutical research, leading to faster research timelines and more dependable results.

Scaling Operations Seamlessly: Agentic AI enables companies to grow without needing to hire more staff in proportion. Businesses who are expanding into new markets, growing quickly, or dealing with seasonal variations in demand will find this scalability especially beneficial. An e-commerce business, for example, can ensure customer pleasure without overtaxing human staff by using AI-powered customer care agents to manage an increase in inquiries during busy shopping seasons.

Agentic AI enables companies to attain greater performance levels while preserving or even lowering operating expenses by improving productivity through resource management, process automation, and predictive capabilities. As a result, autonomous systems increase productivity, allowing businesses to better satisfy customer needs and adjust to shifting market dynamics.

5.3 Changing Work Roles in the Agentic AI Era

The emergence of agentic AI is altering roles and responsibilities in the workplace in addition to how work is completed. Human roles are changing to include more strategic, creative, and interpersonal duties as AI replaces an increasing percentage of routine and analytical activities. In order to create a collaborative atmosphere where AI and human expertise complement one another, this transition necessitates that businesses and individuals adjust to new methods of working.

Transitioning from Task-Oriented to Strategic Positions: Many repetitive jobs can now be handled by agentic AI, freeing up human workers to concentrate on major projects. For instance, data analysts who used to devote a lot of time on organizing and cleaning data can now concentrate more on analyzing insights and offering strategic advice. This change enables human workers to perform higher-level tasks that call for ingenuity, discernment, and long-term planning.

The need for technical and AI-specific skills is growing. The need for workers with technical skills, such as AI literacy, data science, and machine learning, is increasing as AI systems are incorporated into the workplace more and more. Data governance experts, AI ethicists, and AI trainers are becoming vital parts of the contemporary workforce. Workers having these abilities are essential to the creation, administration, and upkeep of AI systems, guaranteeing their moral and efficient operation.

Emphasizing Human-Centric Skills: Emotional intelligence, creativity, and sophisticated problem-solving are examples of distinctly human skills that are becoming more and more valuable in an AI-driven workplace. Data-driven activities might be handled by AI, but jobs requiring empathy, intuition, and interpersonal communication are still vital. For instance, in the medical field, human professionals offer invaluable empathy, patient communication, and nuanced judgment, even though AI can help with diagnoses. In a similar vein, human agents in customer service deal with delicate or complicated matters that call for a customized strategy.

As AI Moves Towards Collaborative Roles: Working directly with AI systems is becoming a distinct part of new employment roles. Employees in industries like marketing, finance, and logistics are working together more and more with AI tools to improve decision-making and results. Marketing experts, for example, may use AI systems to examine consumer behavior and preferences in order to develop tailored advertising campaigns. Through this partnership, human staff members can contribute their knowledge and creativity while utilizing AI's analytical capabilities.

Encouraging Ongoing Education and Flexibility: The abilities needed in the workplace are evolving along with AI technologies. For workers to stay up to date with AI developments, organizations need to foster a culture of lifelong learning. Through training programs, reskilling initiatives, and professional development opportunities, individuals can learn how to properly interact with AI systems and adjust to changing job requirements. Building a resilient workforce that can prosper in an AI-enhanced world requires this learning-focused approach.

Addressing Ethical and Social Implications: The use of AI in the workplace brings up significant ethical issues related to bias, privacy, and job displacement. Organizations are consequently establishing positions tasked with supervising AI ethics, responsible implementation, and regulatory compliance. These positions guarantee that AI systems function within moral bounds and that their implementation takes into account the wider societal effects on workers, clients, and society. An AI ethical officer might, for instance, examine algorithms to make sure that employee data privacy is maintained or to stop discriminatory results.

Job responsibilities are changing to prioritize strategic thinking, creativity, and teamwork in the age of agentic AI. Agentic AI makes the workforce more robust and dynamic by allowing workers to concentrate on high-value tasks and encouraging an adaptable culture. Role changes demonstrate AI's ability to unleash human potential by reorienting attention from repetitive duties to meaningful activity that fosters innovation and advances organizational expansion.

By redefining job responsibilities, increasing efficiency, and offloading chores, agentic AI is radically changing the workplace. AI frees workers from repetitive duties through job offloading and human augmentation, allowing them to concentrate on strategic work. AI increases productivity by maximizing resources and streamlining processes, allowing businesses to accomplish more with less. Furthermore, the incorporation of agentic AI reinterprets roles, encouraging workers to perform more strategic, creative, and cooperative tasks. This change calls for a change in skill sets, with a focus on flexibility, human-centered knowledge, and ongoing education. In the end, agentic AI is transforming the contemporary workplace into a dynamic setting where AI enhances human potential, promoting advancement for both individuals and organizations.

CHAPTER 6

AGENTIC AI SECURITY AND CREDIBILITY

It is crucial to guarantee the security, dependability, and compliance of agentic AI systems as they are progressively included into vital industries. Organizations must proactively address special security risks to guard against potential misuse, vulnerabilities, and ethical dilemmas because of the autonomous nature and decision-making powers of agentic AI. This chapter explores the fundamental procedures for creating reliable, secure AI systems that stakeholders can rely on.

6.1 Making Sure Agentic AI Systems Are Secure and Sturdy

A multi-layered strategy that considers possible risks, foresees weaknesses, and implements safeguards to protect the system and the data it interacts with is necessary to build reliable and secure agentic AI systems. Strong system security is a crucial part of development since agentic AI systems become more vulnerable to security threats as they become more complicated.

Building Resilience Against Cyberattacks: Because agentic AI functions autonomously, these systems are particularly vulnerable to cyberattacks. The ability of a system to endure and bounce back from cyberattacks without losing functioning is known as cyber resilience. Resilience measures can be implemented by agentic AI systems by:

1. **Advanced Encryption:** By encrypting any data that the AI system processes, transmits, or stores, it lessens vulnerability to unwanted access.

2. Only authorized personnel are able to access important functions within the system thanks to role-based access control, which guarantees secure access management.

3. **Real-Time Monitoring and Anomaly Detection:** By incorporating AI-powered cybersecurity solutions that continuously scan for anomalous activity, risks can be identified and eliminated sooner.

Ensuring System Integrity: Integrity safeguards guarantee the dependability and purity of the AI system's actions and outputs. In order to preserve integrity, agentic AI systems ought to:

1. The implementation of robust validation protocols is necessary to guard against malicious injections and inaccurate data that could change the behavior of the system. This is especially true for inputs originating from external sources.

2. **Secure Software Update Mechanisms:** To fix vulnerabilities, regular patches and updates are required. Secure update systems guarantee that updates are unaltered and originate from reliable sources.

Data privacy is an important consideration since agentic AI systems frequently handle private or sensitive data. Among the precautions are:

1. **Data Minimization:** By limiting the amount of data that is collected and kept, possible dangers in the event of a data breach are decreased.

2. **Differential Privacy Techniques:** These methods

guarantee the privacy of personal data by enabling AI models to learn from data without disclosing individual records.

Ensuring Model Robustness: AI models are susceptible to adversarial attacks, in which little changes to the input data can produce unfavorable or erroneous results. Among the methods to improve model robustness are:

1. **Adversarial Training:** AI models are more resistant to manipulation when trained on adversarial cases.
2. Model performance can be proactively improved by conducting regular audits, which lowers the possibility of exploitable vulnerabilities.

A wide range of technical issues must be resolved in order to create secure agentic AI systems. By guaranteeing robustness, resilience, integrity, and privacy, developers build systems that can survive security risks without losing their ability to function.

6.2 Risk Evaluation and Reduction Techniques

For the purpose of detecting possible risks to agentic AI

systems and creating countermeasures, risk assessment is essential. Evaluating system vulnerabilities, estimating possible effects, and developing response strategies to reduce risks are all components of a thorough risk management strategy.

Finding Possible risks: The first step in risk assessment is to find possible external and internal risks that can jeopardize the system. Among these dangers are:

1. The following are examples of external cybersecurity concerns that could jeopardize AI systems: malware, phishing, and unauthorized access.

2. **Internal Risks:** Inadequate access controls, human mistake, and incorrect system configuration can all lead to internal vulnerabilities.

3. **Algorithmic Risks:** Model biases, unforeseen behaviors, or gradual performance deterioration can all impact system dependability.

Quantifying Risk Impact and Likelihood: After possible threats have been identified, determining each risk's probability of happening as well as its possible impact aids in setting priorities for mitigation actions. Risks are categorized as follows:

1. **High Likelihood, High Impact:** Prompt and effective mitigation steps are necessary for risks that are both likely and significant.

2. Even though these hazards are less likely to materialize, they nonetheless require contingency planning in case they do.

3. **High Likelihood, Low Impact:** Simple, preventive measures may be necessary for minor disruptions that are likely to occur but cause little harm.

The development of effective risk mitigation techniques is contingent upon the type and level of identified risks. Typical tactics consist of:

1. **Redundancy and Failover Mechanisms:** Redundancy makes sure that other parts can take over without any problems in the event that one fails.

2. **Regular System Audits and Testing:** Regularly examining the hardware and software components can identify vulnerabilities before they are used against you. Additionally, testing guarantees system

performance in a range of scenarios.

3. Regular backups guarantee that data and functionality may be recovered in the event of a breach or breakdown.

Creating Incident Response Plans: Having a clear incident response plan is crucial when risks cannot be totally avoided. A response strategy ought to consist of:

1. **Immediate Containment Measures:** Damage is reduced when security incidents are contained quickly.

2. **Root Cause Analysis:** Preventing repeated incidents can be achieved by identifying the underlying cause of a security incident.

3. **Post-Incident Recovery and Documentation:** Following containment, restoration of systems and a comprehensive analysis must be recorded for future use.

In addition to increasing the resilience of agentic AI systems, a proactive approach to risk assessment and mitigation gives stakeholders more faith in the system's capacity to manage possible threats.

6.3 AI-Driven Systems: Compliance and Governance

Following ethical governance frameworks and compliance requirements is crucial as agentic AI systems become more and more involved in decision-making. AI systems are guaranteed to function in accordance with organizational, ethical, and legal standards through compliance and governance.

Ensuring Compliance with Legal and Regulatory Standards: In regulated sectors like government, healthcare, and finance, where AI systems must function within predetermined legal bounds, compliance is crucial.

1. **GDPR Compliance for Data Protection:** Agentic AI systems must make sure data processing complies with strict privacy regulations in areas subject to the General Data Protection Regulation (GDPR). This entails protecting private information, getting appropriate consent, and facilitating data mobility.

2. **Industry-Specific Regulations:** To protect sensitive data and uphold transparency, certain industries, such as healthcare and finance, are subject to certain

regulatory standards (e.g., FINRA for finance, and HIPAA for healthcare). To maintain responsibility and confidence, agentic AI systems utilized in these domains must adhere to these guidelines.

The establishment of ethical AI governance frameworks is crucial for directing the moral development, use, and administration of agentic AI systems.

1. **Open Decision-Making Procedures:** Governance frameworks ought to guarantee that decision-making procedures are open and comprehensible. AI systems need to be developed in a way that allows stakeholders to recognize potential biases and comprehend the decision-making process.

2. **Bias Detection and Mitigation:** Because inadvertent biases might result in discriminatory outcomes, AI models need to be routinely assessed for bias. The equitable treatment of all users by AI systems is ensured by methods like bias mitigation algorithms and fairness audits.

3. **Human Oversight and Accountability:** means for human oversight of crucial choices should be in place, and AI systems should answer to human

stakeholders. Clear accountability frameworks offer a means of resolving problems and stop automated judgments from doing harm.

Preserving Transparency via Explainability: Explainability is essential for building confidence in agentic AI systems, particularly in high-stakes applications like law enforcement and healthcare.

1. **Model Interpretability Techniques:** AI model predictions can be made easier to understand by using strategies like SHAP (SHapley Additive exPlanations) and LIME (Local Interpretable Model-Agnostic Explanations). These methods shed light on the ways in which particular factors affect the AI's judgments.

2. **Offering End-User Explanations:** AI systems should give end users intelligible justifications for their choices in order to build confidence. To help physicians comprehend its thinking, a medical diagnostic AI might, for example, provide a justification for the recommended course of treatment.

Continuous Monitoring and Compliance Audits: Adherence to governance frameworks and standards necessitates ongoing audits and monitoring.

1. Frequent compliance audits of AI systems guarantee continuous adherence to changing regulatory requirements.

2. **Automated Monitoring solutions:** AI-powered solutions for monitoring can keep tabs on how the system behaves and notify relevant parties when compliance standards are broken.

Organizations can guarantee that agentic AI systems continue to be moral, open, and responsible by upholding stringent compliance and governance procedures, which will build trust with both users and stakeholders.

Organizations must prioritize strong security measures, thorough risk assessment, and rigorous adherence to ethical and regulatory norms when creating reliable, safe agentic AI systems. Building resilience against cyberthreats, safeguarding data privacy, and upholding system integrity are all necessary to ensure the security of agentic AI. Organizations use risk assessment to find possible weaknesses and put mitigation plans in place to deal with unforeseen circumstances. Frameworks for governance and compliance also guarantee that AI systems function morally and openly, satisfying legal and social demands. Organizations may confidently implement agentic AI, fostering innovation while maintaining safety, trust, and accountability, by giving security, risk management, and governance first priority.

CHAPTER 7

AGENTIC AI's ETHICAL AND SOCIAL CONSEQUENCES

It is crucial to address the ethical and societal ramifications of agentic AI systems as they acquire autonomy and decision-making abilities. Agentic AI's revolutionary potential raises concerns about job displacement, societal effects, accountability, and fairness. To guarantee that agentic AI works in humanity's best interests and within moral bounds, organizations, governments, and developers must overcome these obstacles.

7.1 Juggling Accountability and Autonomy

Achieving a balance between autonomy and accountability is crucial when agentic AI systems assume decision-making responsibilities that have historically been performed by humans. Even while autonomous AI agents can function on their own, they nonetheless need to adhere to the goals and moral principles of their human supervisors. To stop abuse, unforeseen consequences, and moral failings, there must be clear accountability systems in place.

Defining Accountability in Autonomous Systems: In agentic AI, accountability refers to the procedures that hold systems and their creators accountable for the decisions and actions of the AI. Because these systems function independently, figuring out who is responsible can get complicated. For example:

1. **Clear Ownership of AI-Driven Decisions:** When an agentic AI makes a big decision, especially if it causes harm or unintended consequences, developers, organizations, or end users need to specify who is accountable.

2. The establishment of ethical frameworks and rules for agentic AI systems can assist developers in bringing system behavior into line with social norms, promoting the responsible use of AI.

Building Transparent Decision-Making Processes: When AI decision-making is transparent, people can better comprehend the reasoning behind the AI's actions, which facilitates the establishment of accountability. Among the tactics for transparency are:

1. The use of explainable AI techniques, such SHAP (SHapley Additive exPlanations) or LIME (Local Interpretable Model-agnostic Explanations), can shed light on how and why the AI arrived at a specific conclusion.

2. **Human-in-the-Loop Systems:** Human oversight can guarantee that a human reviews and approves final decisions for high-stakes applications. Humans retain control over AI judgments under this hybrid model, particularly in situations where moral or legal issues are crucial.

Providing Redress and Correction Mechanisms: As agentic AI systems become more autonomous, it becomes essential to set up processes for fixing errors or poor decisions. Mechanisms for effective reparation include:

1. **Feedback Loops for Continuous Learning:** By letting users or other impacted parties offer input on AI choices, future mistakes can be reduced and system advancements can continue.

2. **Systems for Reporting and Correcting Errors:**

Organizations should have procedures in place to fix mistakes, compensate impacted parties if needed, and modify the AI's settings to stop recurrence when an AI-driven decision has unfavorable effects.

It takes a multifaceted strategy that includes explicit ownership, openness, and redressal methods to strike a balance between autonomy and accountability. Developers can reduce the dangers associated with autonomous AI behaviors by incorporating accountability measures.

7.2 Handling Fairness and Bias in Self-Determination

From employment procedures to criminal justice, agentic AI systems are frequently used in settings where impartiality and fairness are crucial. On the other hand, biases in the algorithms themselves or in the training data may be reflected in AI models. Building trust in agentic AI systems requires addressing bias and guaranteeing justice in autonomous decision-making.

Identifying and Mitigating Algorithmic Bias: Selective sampling, skewed data, and subjective human input are some of the causes of bias in AI models. In order to effectively manage prejudice, one must:

1. **Bias Detection and Audit Processes:** Agentic AI models undergo routine audits to help detect possible biases before they become harmful. The consistency of results across demographic groupings can be evaluated using techniques such as fairness tests.

2. **Fairness-Aware Algorithms:** By taking into consideration a variety of demographic factors, some algorithms are made to encourage equity. These algorithms make sure that certain groups aren't disproportionately impacted by the AI's decisions.

3. **Data Diversity and Quality:** By covering a broad range of people and situations, the use of high-quality, varied training data reduces bias. Bias can be further minimized by using data preprocessing methods like data balancing.

Ensuring Fair Decision-Making Criteria: Consistent and equitable criteria ought to serve as the foundation for autonomous AI decisions. Establishing moral and equitable guidelines for the AI's operation is necessary to guarantee fair AI.

1. **Determining Objective criteria for Assessment**: By establishing clear, consistent criteria that adhere to fairness norms, objectivity in AI can be strengthened.

2. The criteria employed by agentic AI systems should be reviewed and updated on a regular basis by businesses to ensure that they are in line with current ethical standards. This is because society norms are constantly changing.

Creating Ethical Protections Against Discriminatory Results: Discriminatory AI results might have detrimental effects on society and reputation. Effective anti-discrimination measures include:

1. The implementation of real-time bias monitoring enables firms to identify biased decisions in real-time and take corrective action.

2. **Bias Mitigation Frameworks:** Organizations and developers can use formalized frameworks for bias mitigation to help them create agentic AI that supports equity.

From data selection to algorithm development, attention

must be paid to bias and fairness in agentic AI. Organizations can increase user trust and protect against moral problems in autonomous decision-making by fostering fairness.

7.3 Workforce Transition and Societal Impacts

The widespread use of agentic AI has significant social ramifications, impacting human interaction, economic productivity, and employment trends. Even if AI has many advantages, there are drawbacks to its adoption, especially in terms of labor displacement and the possible loss of some job categories. The advantages of agentic AI can be maximized while reducing its disruptions with a careful strategy to labor transition and society adaptation.

Comprehending the Economic Impact of Agentic AI: The capacity of agentic AI to automate intricate processes and boost productivity offers substantial financial advantages, such as cost reductions, efficiency improvements, and innovation. Important economic effects include:

1. **Enhanced Productivity and Competitiveness:**

Autonomous AI systems improve overall productivity by streamlining procedures, lowering mistake rates, and increasing operational efficiency.

2. **Economic Disparities and Wealth Distribution:** The economic benefits of agentic AI might favor some industries or geographical areas more than others, which could lead to a rise in income inequality.

Tackling Workforce Displacement and Job Evolution: The workforce will have to adjust as AI systems increasingly handle jobs that were previously completed by people. Some employment will be lost as a result of this change, but opportunities in other industries will also arise.

1. Governments and companies should invest in initiatives that assist workers in acquiring new skills pertinent to AI-driven industries in order to ease the transition. These programs involve skill development relating to AI, digital literacy, and technical training.

2. New job roles in AI design, management, and ethics are created as a result of the development of agentic AI. The increased capabilities of agentic AI systems

will be supported by new positions including data scientists, AI operations managers, and ethics officers.

3. **Hybrid Work Environments:** Agentic AI also makes it possible for humans and computers to work together, resulting in hybrid jobs that blend AI-driven insights with human judgment.

Encouraging Ethical Societal Integration of Agentic AI: Ethical considerations that weigh the advantages and disadvantages of AI are necessary for successful societal integration. Among the tactics for ethical integration are:

1. Building trust and fostering reasonable expectations are two benefits of educating the public about the function and limitations of artificial intelligence. Initiatives for public awareness can dispel myths about AI and demystify it.

2. **Ethical Standards and Regulatory Oversight:** Governments are involved in creating rules that create moral limits for AI usage. Regulations on the application of AI in delicate fields, like law enforcement and healthcare, can guard against abuse and guarantee public safety.

3. **Involving Stakeholders:** Developers, legislators, and social scientists working together can guarantee that the creation of agentic AI takes into account a range of viewpoints and societal demands.

Agentic AI has a multifaceted social impact that includes employment, ethical, and economic ramifications. Society may fully grasp the potential of agentic AI while reducing its problems by supporting ethical integration, advancing public education, and preparing for the job shift.

Agentic AI's ethical and social ramifications underscore the necessity of vigilant supervision, conscientious growth, and proactive societal adjustment. By striking a balance between responsibility and autonomy, AI systems can function autonomously while yet being subject to human supervision. A key component of widespread social acceptability is preventing discriminatory outcomes and fostering trust through addressing prejudice and advancing fairness in autonomous AI judgments. Last but not least, society may capitalize on AI's advantages without compromising human welfare by comprehending the societal effects of agentic AI, such as changes in the workforce, changes in the economy, and ethical issues.

Stakeholders can build a future where agentic AI not only spurs innovation but also reflects the ideals of justice, accountability, and social responsibility by giving these ethical and social aspects top priority.

CHAPTER 8

AGENTIC AI IMPLEMENTATION: DIFFICULTIES AND SOLUTIONS

Organizations face substantial challenges when implementing agentic AI systems. To have the greatest possible impact, these systems which are intended to function with a high degree of autonomy need sophisticated technical skills, flexible organizational structures, and an open cultural perspective. The main technical issues that come up while creating autonomous AI systems are covered in this chapter, along with organizational and cultural obstacles that may prevent acceptance and best practices and solutions that can help ensure successful deployment.

8.1 The Development of Autonomous Systems Presents Technical Difficulties

Beyond those of conventional AI models, the technological

difficulties of deploying agentic AI systems call for sophisticated approaches, strong frameworks, and a dedication to ongoing learning and adaptation. The intricacy of autonomous decision-making, real-time processing requirements, and secure integration are just a few of the challenges that developers must overcome.

Difficulty in Goal-Driven and Autonomous Decision-Making: One of the technological challenges is creating AI systems that can make decisions on their own while still adhering to organizational objectives.

1. **Goal Alignment:** It takes sophisticated programming and reinforcement learning strategies to make sure the AI's behaviors match the desired goals. To direct the AI's decision-making, developers frequently use complex reward functions and limitations.

2. **Balancing Autonomy with Oversight:** The difficulty is in developing transparent, autonomous systems that allow human supervisors to comprehend and step in when needed. For traceability and accountability, it is essential to incorporate explainable AI (XAI) capabilities into

these systems.

3. **Adaptability**: When their surroundings change, autonomous systems need to react quickly. AI bots may adapt without requiring manual reprogramming thanks to methods like online reinforcement learning and constant learning.

Data Quality and Real-Time Processing: Real-time information processing and high-quality data are critical to agentic AI's efficacy.

1. **Data Reliability:** In autonomous systems, inaccurate, skewed, or out-of-date data can result in poor decision-making that has far-reaching effects. Strict data validation, filtering, and frequent updates are necessary to guarantee data trustworthiness.

2. **Real-Time Analysis**: AI is necessary for many applications to process data rapidly. For instance, real-time data processing is necessary for robotic systems and driverless cars to make snap choices. This calls for the creation of hardware solutions and quick, effective algorithms that enable real-time execution.

Assuring Robustness and Security: Agentic AI systems frequently function independently in unpredictably changing situations where malfunction or intervention might have dire consequences, therefore robustness and security are essential.

1. **System Resilience:** Autonomous AI systems need to be able to withstand a wide range of unanticipated events. To make sure the system can withstand unforeseen inputs or circumstances, this resilience frequently entails thorough testing and the usage of simulation environments.

2. **Cybersecurity:** Cyberattacks have the potential to compromise data, interfere with services, or influence decisions in autonomous systems, particularly those that are online. To protect against these dangers, safe data handling procedures, end-to-end encryption, and AI-driven security measures are crucial.

For agentic AI systems to be dependable, secure, and effective, several technological obstacles must be overcome. Strong goal alignment, high-quality data, real-time processing, and rigorous security measures enable enterprises to create autonomous systems that are technically sound and operate well in challenging environments.

8.2 Cultural and Organizational Adoption Barriers

The success of the adoption of agentic AI is largely dependent on organizational and cultural variables, even in the case of technically solid AI systems. The integration of agentic AI into current workflows may be hampered by cultural worries about AI autonomy, resistance to change, and a lack of AI literacy.

Resistance to Change and Fear of Job Displacement: Employees frequently experience anxiety and resistance when autonomous AI systems alter job roles and workflows.

1. Employees may worry about losing their jobs as a result of AI-driven automation that can replace some tasks. These worries may result in a lack of collaboration, a decline in morale, or even overt opposition to AI projects.

2. Employee responsibilities may change from task

execution to supervision and strategic planning as AI systems take on increasingly complicated duties. Time, training, and an organizationally flexible mentality are all necessary for this shift.

Lack of AI Literacy and Skills Gap: Implementation efforts may be hampered by a workforce that is not familiar with AI concepts and finds it difficult to adjust to agentic AI.

1. The implementation of autonomous AI systems frequently necessitates the acquisition of new skills, specifically in data analysis, system monitoring, and ethical AI practices. In order to close the knowledge gap, funding upskilling initiatives is essential.

2. The strategic ramifications and constraints of agentic AI must also be understood by organizational leaders and stakeholders. AI projects run the danger of being mishandled or underestimated in the absence of senior support and clear direction.

Cultural Issues and Ethical Ambiguity: Because of its capacity for autonomous decision-making, agentic AI presents ethical questions about accountability, control, and reliability.

1. **Trust in Autonomous Decision-Making**: It can be difficult to establish confidence in AI systems that make decisions on their own, especially when no human supervision is present. Giving power to computers may arouse skepticism among stakeholders and employees, particularly in high-stakes situations.

2. **Managing Ethical Ambiguities:** The use of AI in decision-making brings up issues of moral responsibility. Companies must establish moral standards for agentic AI systems, especially when the results of AI directly affect workers or clients.

It takes meticulous preparation, communication, and a dedication to transparency to overcome organizational and cultural barriers. Organizations can help make the adoption of agentic AI systems go more smoothly by encouraging a culture of continuous learning and actively involve staff members in the shift.

8.3 Best Practices and Solutions for Effective Implementation

A strategic strategy that takes organizational, ethical, and technical factors into account is necessary for the successful deployment of agentic AI systems. Establishing ethical principles, investing in infrastructure and training, and encouraging stakeholder alignment are some solutions and best practices.

Encouraging Stakeholder Alignment and Collaboration: From executives to frontline staff, alignment across all organizational levels is essential for a successful AI deployment.

1. **Create a Clear AI Strategy:** Companies should create a clear AI strategy that includes objectives, aims, and expected effects. A clear plan guarantees that everyone involved is aware of the benefits and goals of agentic AI, which lowers opposition and fosters collaboration.

2. **Cross-Functional Collaboration:** Diverse viewpoints and cooperation are promoted by involving people from several departments, such as

operations, HR, and IT. Cross-functional teams are able to recognize possible problems and work together to create solutions that benefit the entire company.

Investing in Infrastructure and Upskilling: The effective deployment and operation of autonomous AI systems depend on technical infrastructure and staff training.

1. **Creating Scalable and Reliable Infrastructure:** Agentic AI systems frequently need sophisticated infrastructure that can manage real-time analytics and massive data processing. These needs are supported and scalability is made possible by cloud platforms, edge computing, and data centers built for AI workloads.

2. **Initiatives for AI literacy and upskilling program**s: To prepare the workforce to collaborate with agentic AI systems, training on AI-related ideas, resources, and ethical issues is crucial. To guarantee that skills stay current, training should incorporate practical exercises, certifications, and continuing education.

Creating Ethical and Governance Frameworks: Ethical governance offers a framework for the appropriate application of agentic AI, guaranteeing that systems function within socially acceptable bounds and in accordance with principles.

1. **Creating Ethical rules:** Companies should create ethical rules that outline acceptable conduct and limits for AI that operates on its own. This contributes to the development of public trust by establishing standards for openness, equity, and data privacy.

2. **AI Governance Committees**: To guarantee continuous evaluation and adherence to moral principles, an AI governance committee or other comparable oversight body should be established. These committees are able to oversee AI performance, control risk, and deal with moral dilemmas as they emerge.

3. **Regular Audits and Compliance Checks:** Consistent auditing of AI systems guarantees compliance with industry rules and ethical standards. Organizations can take proactive measures to remedy problems by using compliance checks to

find any biases, mistakes, or hazards.

Implementing Continuous Monitoring and Feedback Loops: To sustain performance and goal alignment, autonomous systems benefit from continuous review.

1. **Real-Time Monitoring:** Organizations may track AI performance continually with real-time monitoring solutions, which enables quick responses to unforeseen problems or faults.

2. **User Feedback Channels:** Promoting end-user input yields insightful information about AI functionality and user experience. Over time, this feedback can enhance system functionality and guide incremental improvements.

3. **Adaptive Learning Mechanisms:** Agentic AI systems can enhance their performance and adapt to novel situations on their own thanks to adaptive learning. These systems are able to adapt to changes in their surroundings or user requirements by means of ongoing learning and model updates.

Organizations may overcome the difficulties of implementing agentic AI and create systems that are not only technically sound but also morally and socially acceptable by adhering to these solutions and best practices.

Putting agentic AI systems into practice is a complex process that requires overcoming organizational, cultural, and technical obstacles. Building dependable systems requires overcoming technical obstacles like maintaining strong security and enabling real-time decision-making. Clear communication, stakeholder engagement, and staff upskilling programs can help reduce organizational and cultural opposition, which is frequently based on worries about job loss and a lack of AI literacy.

Organizations should follow a structured approach that prioritizes infrastructure investment, ethical governance, stakeholder alignment, and ongoing monitoring in order to guarantee successful implementation. Organizations can embrace the revolutionary power of agentic AI while maintaining ethical standards and preparing their workforce for an AI-augmented future by cultivating collaboration and establishing a culture of trust. Agentic AI can be successfully incorporated with careful planning and proactive management, allowing enterprises to accomplish their objectives in a sustainable and responsible way.

CHAPTER 9

AGENTIC AI FORECASTS AND FUTURE TRENDS

Because it is autonomous and goal-driven, agentic AI has the potential to revolutionize a variety of fields, society, and even the structure of human-machine interactions. Organizations, legislators, and technologists can use a number of new trends and forecasts to help them comprehend and get ready for the changing role of agentic AI. The potential of agentic AI by 2028 and beyond, its convergence with other disruptive technologies, and strategies for preparing for its long-term societal and organizational impact will all be covered in this chapter, along with insights from Gartner and other market analysts.

9.1 Gartner Projects the Development of Agentic AI by 2028 and Later

Leading industry analysts, like Gartner, predict that agentic AI will soon dominate a variety of industries. It is anticipated that the widespread use of agentic AI would result in major changes to worker dynamics, organizational structures, and consumer interaction by 2028.

Increased Adoption in Industry: According to Gartner, agentic AI will be widely used in a variety of industries by 2028, including manufacturing, logistics, healthcare, and finance. The ability of agentic AI to carry out intricate activities on its own, streamline processes, and facilitate effective decision-making without the need for human participation will lead to this trend.

1. **customized Medicine and Healthcare**: Agentic AI is anticipated to propel customized medicine in the healthcare industry by independently evaluating patient data, suggesting therapies, and spotting possible health hazards before they become apparent. With AI systems actively participating in health monitoring and lifestyle modifications, this capability may result in preventive care being the standard.

2. **Finance and Autonomous Trading:** Agentic AI has the potential to take over algorithmic trading, credit risk evaluation, and fraud detection in the finance

industry. These technologies could assist businesses in making better, quicker financial decisions, lowering risk and increasing profitability, by independently evaluating current market patterns and financial data.

Transformative Workforce Changes: It is projected that agentic AI will play a major role in transforming the workforce by 2028. Job roles may change as a result of agentic AI's capacity to do activities independently, rendering some obsolete and giving rise to new, AI-focused professions.

1. **Redefinition of Roles:** As agentic AI takes over routine and repetitive work, these positions are expected to disappear, while roles centered on ethical governance, AI oversight, and innovative problem-solving will increase. Because of this change, companies will need to actively retrain their employees in higher-level capabilities and AI literacy.

2. **Enhanced Productivity:** Human workers will have more time to concentrate on strategic planning, creative work, and interpersonal duties while agentic

AI systems take care of time-consuming, repetitive activities. According to Gartner, this augmentation will result in a significant boost in workforce productivity overall, with AI and human collaboration reaching unprecedented levels.

The Emergence of AI-Driven firms: According to Gartner, many firms will transition to an "AI-driven" operational model by 2028, in which a significant amount of daily tasks, decision-making, and data processing will be controlled by agentic AI systems. It is anticipated that this tendency would radically alter customer relations and organizational structures.

1. **Scale Data-Driven Decision-Making:** AI-driven businesses will give data-driven insights top priority when making important decisions. Because AI systems can analyze large volumes of data, identify patterns, and recommend or carry out actions on their own, agentic AI will speed up, improve accuracy, and reduce human error in decision-making processes.

2. **Customer-Centric Experiences:** Agentic AI will be used by businesses more and more to provide

real-time, customized customer experiences. Retail businesses, for example, might use agentic AI to automatically handle pricing, inventory, and customer service, giving each consumer a more personalized and responsive experience.

Organizations may prepare themselves for a future in which agentic AI plays a key role in operations and decision-making by comprehending these trends and creating strategies that match Gartner's predictions.

9.2 Integration with Additional Up-and-Coming Technologies

Agentic AI will have a greater impact and open up new avenues for innovation when it converges with other cutting-edge technologies. It is anticipated that technologies like blockchain, the Internet of Things (IoT), and quantum computing will work in concert with agentic AI to expand the capabilities of autonomous systems.

The integration of blockchain technology with agentic artificial intelligence (AI) has the potential to improve data security, integrity, and transparency all of which are critical for fostering confidence in autonomous systems.

1. **Secure Data Sharing:** Without a centralized middleman, blockchain's decentralized ledger technology enables safe, traceable data exchange across AI systems. In sectors where data security and privacy are critical, such as healthcare, banking, and supply chain management, this capacity can be especially helpful.

2. **Auditable AI Transactions:** Blockchain technology can offer an unchangeable log of AI decisions and actions, allowing businesses to examine AI conduct in the past. Concerns of trust and responsibility are addressed by this integration, particularly in contexts where agentic AI functions independently.

Real-time, on-site decision-making across linked devices and systems will be facilitated by the integration of agentic AI with IoT and edge computing.

1. **Real-Time Autonomy:** Agentic AI can make quick, local decisions without depending on cloud-based resources by processing data locally on IoT devices (via edge computing). This feature is especially

useful in situations involving industrial automation, smart cities, and driverless cars.

2. **Enhanced Data Collection:** Massive volumes of real-time data are produced by IoT networks, which are made up of sensors and connected devices. By using this data, agentic AI may make well-informed judgments on its own, increasing efficiency in energy management, resource distribution, and other areas.

Quantum Computing: Although it is still in its infancy, quantum computing has the potential to greatly enhance agentic AI by processing intricate calculations and extensive optimizations more quickly than traditional computing.

1. **Accelerating Machine Learning:** Agentic AI could examine large datasets and extract insights in a matter of seconds if quantum computing greatly accelerates machine learning methods. Such speed could improve the ability of autonomous decision-making, particularly in sectors like emergency services and finance that need quick reactions.

2. **Resolving Optimization Issues:** When paired with quantum computing, agentic AI can more effectively manage intricate optimization tasks, like supply chain logistics and real-time traffic control, leading to improved performance in dynamic contexts.

These integrations are not without their difficulties, such as the requirement for new infrastructure investments and interdisciplinary knowledge. Organizations that strategically combine these technologies with agentic AI, however, have the potential to achieve hitherto unheard-of levels of autonomy in operations.

9.3 Getting Ready for Agentic AI's Long-Term Effects

Although there are many advantages to agentic AI, there are also long-term issues and ramifications that call for serious thought and preparation. Addressing ethical issues, developing governance structures, and encouraging flexibility across sectors and communities are all part of preparing for its effects.

The establishment of ethical and regulatory frameworks

will be crucial for preserving accountability, transparency, and public trust as agentic AI takes on greater decision-making responsibilities.

Governments, businesses, and AI developers must collaborate to establish ethical norms and guidelines that outline appropriate AI conduct, accountability procedures, and sanctions for abuse.

Organizations ought to put in place AI governance models that supervise agentic AI operations and make sure they adhere to moral principles. Regular monitoring, audits, and the appointment of Chief AI Ethics Officers and other ethical AI positions within companies are all part of this.

The long-term effects of agentic AI will cause major shifts in the dynamics of the workforce, necessitating the development of new skill sets and adaptable mindsets.

1. **Upskilling and Reskilling Initiatives:** Companies need to make a commitment to ongoing education programs that assist staff in acquiring skills that go hand in hand with agentic AI. Digital literacy, data analysis, problem-solving, and creative thinking are all included in this.

2. The workforce will increasingly concentrate on

higher-level duties including supervision, strategic planning, and ethical issues as agentic AI automates repetitive activities. Roles should be redesigned to match these changing duties as an organization gets ready for this change.

Resolving Social and Economic Disruption: The widespread use of agentic AI could result in social and economic upheavals, such as adjustments to employment trends and disparities in income.

1. **Government Policies and Social Programs**: In order to support impacted workers, policymakers must foresee future job market disruptions and implement measures like retraining programs, unemployment insurance, and job creation projects in AI-augmented positions.

2. **Universal Basic Income (UBI):** According to some economists, UBI could be a way to lessen the financial burden of job displacement brought on by AI. As the workforce shifts to new occupations in the AI-driven economy, universal basic income (UBI) would ensure financial stability by giving everyone a guaranteed income.

In order to make informed decisions and promote a responsible AI ecosystem, it is imperative that the general public have a basic understanding of AI as agentic AI becomes more common.

1. **Educational Initiatives:** By updating curricula, holding public lectures, and launching awareness campaigns, governments and educational establishments may encourage AI literacy. Understanding AI's potential, constraints, and moral ramifications will aid society in comprehending and navigating its revolutionary impacts.

2. **Public-Private Partnerships:** Public-private sector cooperation can propel educational programs, guaranteeing that AI literacy is current and available to a variety of demographics.

By taking proactive measures to address the long-term effects of agentic AI, communities, governments, and organizations can foster a future in which AI is used ethically and fairly to benefit society. Social regulations, workforce flexibility, and ethical standards will be crucial in ensuring that agentic AI fulfills its potential while lowering risks and interruptions.

Agentic AI has a bright future ahead of it, but it also presents many difficult obstacles. According to Gartner's predictions, agentic AI will revolutionize many industries by 2028, reshaping workflows and organizations. Agentic AI's capabilities will be further enhanced by integration with cutting-edge technologies like blockchain, IoT, and quantum computing, opening up new avenues for optimization and autonomy. To ensure that AI develops responsibly and serves all stakeholders, it is necessary to address ethical, regulatory, workforce, and social issues in order to be ready for the long-term effects of agentic AI.

CHAPTER 10

THE WAY AHEAD: TECHNIQUES FOR CIOS AND COMPANY EXECUTIVES

CIOs and business executives must make important choices regarding how to plan, measure, and foster an AI-driven future as more and more companies seek to incorporate agentic AI into their operations. Adopting technology is only one aspect of implementing agentic AI; another is changing how businesses operate, compete, and generate value. With an emphasis on strategic planning, impact measures, and creating a resilient, flexible, and effective AI-driven company, this chapter provides CIOs and business executives with practical tools to help them traverse this revolutionary path.

10.1 Agentic AI Integration Strategic Planning

The foundation of an effective adoption of agentic AI is strategic planning. Managing the challenges of integrating autonomous AI systems while creating a plan that supports long-term corporate objectives is crucial for CIOs and company executives. Choosing the appropriate technologies for implementation, comprehending the corporate environment, and establishing specific goals are all components of strategic planning.

Set Clearly Defined Business Goals: Business executives must set clear goals for how agentic AI will benefit the company before starting the AI integration process. These goals must to be connected to more general company objectives like:

1. **Operational Efficiency:** How would agentic AI increase productivity, lower expenses, and automate procedures?

2. **Innovation and Market Positioning:** How can AI support the company's efforts to innovate its offerings in terms of goods, services, and customer satisfaction?

3. **Growth and Scalability:** How will agentic AI affect the company's capacity to expand operations, penetrate new markets, and adjust to emerging trends?

Assessing organizational readiness is important since implementing agentic AI is a big change. To ascertain preparedness for integrating AI, CIOs should evaluate the workforce's skills, operational procedures, and present technology environment. The following are important questions to answer:

1. **Technology Infrastructure:** Does the company have the data management systems, cloud services, and processing power required to support agentic AI?

2. **Data Availability and Quality:** Can AI systems interpret and make judgments on their own using clean, organized data?

3. **Skill Sets and Culture:** Does the company have AI talent on staff, and is there a collaborative and innovative culture to encourage the adoption of AI?

Prioritize Use Cases and Pilot Programs: Because agentic AI is complicated, leaders should give priority to high-impact use cases that support corporate objectives and show how AI can provide real benefits. Before expanding, companies can test and improve AI integration in a controlled setting by starting with pilot initiatives. The following are typical use cases for pilot programs:

1. The implementation of AI-powered chatbots and virtual assistants to enhance customer service response times and personalization is known as "customer service automation."

2. **Supply Chain Optimization:** Managing inventories, logistics, and demand forecasting autonomously with agentic AI.

3. **Financial Decision-Making:** Using AI-powered algorithms to manage risk evaluations, fraud detection, and financial transactions.

Long-Term Vision and Flexibility: CIOs need to anticipate future advancements in AI technology and changing market situations in order to implement AI, even while immediate use cases are crucial. Maintaining the organization's agility and competitiveness requires a flexible AI strategy that can be adjusted to new developments or unanticipated obstacles.

10.2 Metrics to Assess Success and Impact

A strong framework for evaluating the effectiveness and impact of AI efforts is necessary for the successful integration of agentic AI within an enterprise. This focuses on the larger organizational transformation brought about by AI rather than just monitoring simple indicators like acceptance rates and implementation costs.

Metrics for Operational Efficiency: Increasing operational efficiency is one of the main motivations for putting agentic AI into practice. Improvements in important operational areas should be measured in order to assess AI's efficacy:

1. **Time Savings and Process Automation:** How much time is saved by automating repetitive operations and procedures? Cycle time reduction, quicker decision-making, and bottleneck removal are metrics to monitor here.

2. **Cost Reduction:** In what ways does AI lower operating expenses? This could include financial savings from lower labor expenses, less waste, and fewer process failures.

3. Agentic AI is capable of optimizing the allocation of resources. AI's operational impact can be quantified

by tracking improvements in resource usage, such as energy use, inventory control, and worker productivity.

Business Growth KPIs: Agentic AI's contribution to business growth and innovation must be monitored in addition to operational KPIs. The following are some key performance indicators (KPIs) for this field:

1. **Growth in Revenue:** Has artificial intelligence (AI) boosted revenue through better sales results, new AI-driven goods and services, or more customer engagement?

2. **Market Share**: How has the company gained a competitive edge, entered new markets, or provided unique services as a result of implementing agentic AI?

3. **Loyalty and Customer Satisfaction:** Measuring customer satisfaction, Net Promoter Scores (NPS), and retention rates can give insights into how AI affects client relationships, especially when it comes to AI-powered enhancements in the customer experience, including personalized care and predictive support.

AI Performance Metrics: Organizations should monitor AI-specific performance metrics in order to evaluate the technical success of agentic AI:

1. **Accuracy and Reliability:** Do the AI systems regularly produce correct results and make trustworthy data-driven decisions? For predictive models, error rates, precision, and recall are important measures.

2. **Autonomy Level:** How well does the AI function on its own without assistance from humans? The maturity of AI systems can be measured by monitoring the proportion of decisions that are made automatically vs those that need human supervision.

3. **Scalability:** Does the AI system's performance hold steady as its use and complexity increase? System uptime, latency, and the capacity to handle growing data quantities are examples of scalability measures.

Employee and Cultural Impact: Although AI's commercial and technology effects are important, employee acceptance, teamwork, and organizational culture alignment are also crucial for AI initiatives to succeed.

1. **Employee Engagement and Adoption Rates:** Monitoring employee use of AI tools and adoption rates can reveal information about how widely AI systems are accepted.

2. **Training and Reskilling Success:** In order to assess workforce readiness, metrics pertaining to the effectiveness of employee training programs, such as the quantity of workers who have gained advanced skills in AI tools and their performance after training, are essential.

3. **Cultural Alignment**: Assessing how AI adoption fits into the business's creativity, teamwork, and change management culture can assist in determining whether the company is prepared for a future driven by AI.

10.3 Creating an AI-Powered Organization That Is Robust, Flexible, and Effective

The ability of the company to adjust, develop, and sustain productivity in a quickly shifting environment is essential for the successful integration of agentic AI. Business executives must concentrate on creating an atmosphere where AI technologies enhance human creativity and provide lasting value if they want to develop an AI-driven organization that is robust, flexible, and productive.

Cultivating a Culture of Continuous Learning: Creating a culture of continuous learning that encourages staff members to learn new skills and adjust to new technologies is essential to creating a resilient AI-driven company.

1. **Upskilling and Reskilling Initiatives:** To guarantee that staff members are equipped to collaborate with AI systems, organizations need to make continuous training program investments. This involves offering classes in machine learning, data science, AI literacy, and moral AI practices.

2. **AI as a Collaborative collaborator:** AI should be seen as a collaborator that can enhance human abilities rather than as a substitute for human talent. Promoting this way of thinking results in a more positive working relationship between AI and workers, which boosts output and creativity.

Agile Organizational Structures: Businesses need to

embrace flexibility and agility in their operations if they want to prosper in an AI-driven environment. To do this, teams must use agile approaches that enable quick testing, iteration, and scaling of AI projects.

1. **Cross-Disciplinary Collaboration:** Diverse teams, including IT, data science, business operations, and human resources, must work together to implement agentic AI. To make sure AI systems complement corporate objectives, leaders should dismantle silos and promote interdisciplinary cooperation.

2. **Decentralized Decision-Making:** Teams can become more responsive and efficient when given the freedom to decide for themselves. Routine choices can be handled by AI systems, freeing up human leaders to concentrate on higher-level strategy and make the company more flexible.

Building Resilience Against AI hazards: Organizations must take into consideration the hazards associated with autonomous systems as they integrate agentic AI. Developing precautions and backup plans to reduce possible hazards is necessary to provide resilience.

1. Organizations should set up explicit governance

frameworks that supervise AI operations and guarantee moral decision-making in order to mitigate the hazards related to AI autonomy. This could involve risk management plans, ongoing audits, and AI ethical committees.

2. Despite the fact that agentic AI is intended to be independent, it is crucial to be ready for any unforeseen setbacks. For AI judgments to stay in line with corporate objectives and moral principles, organizations should put in place fail-safes, rollback procedures, and human monitoring systems.

In order to optimize AI-driven productivity, companies must make sure that AI tools are smoothly incorporated into processes, removing any conflict between human teams and AI systems.

1. **Workflow Automation:** To free up staff members to concentrate on more strategic endeavors, agentic AI should be integrated into workflows to automate repetitive chores.

2. **Performance Monitoring:** AI systems are always operating at their peak efficiency when performance is continuously monitored and workflows are

modified to maximize productivity.

By using these tactics, CIOs and company executives can successfully negotiate the challenges of integrating agentic AI, guaranteeing that AI turns into a useful tool that improves organizational productivity, resilience, and flexibility. The future of AI-driven businesses is not one in which humans are replaced by computers, but rather one in which long-term success, innovation, and exponential development are the results of intelligent collaboration.

ABOUT THE AUTHOR

 Author and thought leader in the IT field Taylor Royce is well known. He has a two-decade career and is an expert at tech trend analysis and forecasting, which enables a wide audience to understand complicated concepts.

Royce's considerable involvement in the IT industry stemmed from his passion with technology, which he developed during his computer science studies. He has extensive knowledge of the industry because of his experience in both software development and strategic consulting.

Known for his research and lucidity, he has written multiple best-selling books and contributed to esteemed tech periodicals. Translations of Royce's books throughout the world demonstrate his impact.

Royce is a well-known authority on emerging technologies and their effects on society, frequently requested as a speaker at international conferences and as a guest on tech podcasts. He promotes the development of ethical technology, emphasizing problems like data privacy and the digital divide.

In addition, with a focus on sustainable industry growth, Royce mentors upcoming tech experts and supports IT education projects. Taylor Royce is well known for his ability to combine analytical thinking with technical know-how. He sees a time when technology will ethically benefit humanity.